Covenant with God

a Biblical and Historical View at Healing Our Nation

DAVID L. MAHAN

ISBN 979-8-88943-536-5 (paperback)
ISBN 979-8-88943-537-2 (digital)

Christian Faith Publishing
832 Park Avenue
Meadville, PA 16335
www.christianfaithpublishing.com

Printed in the United States of America

To my dear family—my wife, Brandy; my son Joshua; and my two sisters, Deborah and Ellen, for their ever-faithful and unconditional love and support

Also, many thanks to the three men who helped shape my foundation of faith and conviction, all in heaven now—Lee Mahan (my dad), Dr. C. Peter Wagner, and Pastor Jack Hayford.

Introduction

It was not my intent to write this book as a means of proselytizing the reader to Christianity. It is my intent, however, and heartfelt prayer that this book will serve as a wake-up call to America to stop being divisive, abandon the destructive rhetoric, cease the victim entitlement mindset, eliminate the sanctimonious posturing, and return to the Judeo-Christian values and the covenant with God our Founding Fathers cherished so dearly. My hope is that this warning cry will stimulate an awakening, similar to the ones in our history, such as the religious revival that impacted the colonies in America during the 1730s and 1740s known as the Great Awakening, as well as the Azusa Street Revival in the Los Angeles area from April 9, 1906, until roughly 1909. These dispensational movements came at a time when the notion of secular rationalism was being emphasized and passion for religious ideals and values had become stagnant.

However, it's not religion that I want to focus on in this book but rather a covenant agreement that comes from a life-giving relationship with the Almighty God.

Chapter 1

Covenant Promise

As I begin this humble endeavor, I am compelled to admonish the reader that if one does not hold to the firm belief in God as Creator and Giver of Life and does not share the conviction that the Bible is the authoritative Word of God, then that person may not find this book of significant value. However, if the reader, whether Jew or Gentile, cherishes the Word of God and believes in the sovereignty of the Almighty, then I pray this book will help stir a deeper conviction of what must be corrected if our great nation is to be saved. May the LORD bless you and keep you as you receive this simple reminder.

Growing up in a family of ministers, from the "greatest generation," I was taught at a very early age the nonnegotiable fundamental belief in keeping one's promise. It was inculcated in my mind that a man's, or woman's, word is truly the most important attribute of their character. It literally defines their integrity and moral compass.

My father instilled in my two sisters and me the impetus that became the foundation of every decision we would ever make—"be sure to keep your commitments." We knew there would be severe consequences if we broke a promise to someone, most of all loss of our own credibility, as well as our family's. It was inherently engrained within us the concept of being connected to our family unit and even beyond our sphere of influence. The big idea was that my failings would have a ripple effect that would impact others around me, perhaps even in ways perceived as innocuous at first.

Then as I grew in the faith and learned the Holy Scriptures, it became very apparent where my father received such convictions. One doesn't have to look far in the Bible to see that the very foundation of God's character and nature is His Word. I remember the first time reading 2 Samuel 21:1–14 and learning of how "there was a great famine in the land, and David inquired of the LORD as to the cause."

As I read on, I discovered it was due to a broken covenant between the people of Israel and a tribe known as the Gibeonites. When the Israelites were taking possession of the promised land many years before, they had made a promise before God to spare the Gibeonites and allow them to live among the people of Israel. They promised them provision and protection. However, years later, Saul, in his thirst for power, decided to kill many of the Gibeonites. God revealed to David that the broken covenant was the sole cause of the famine cursing the land. After all, *covenants are viewed as the most sacred and binding of deals—an oath that's never to be broken.*

Before I continue to recount this story, I feel it incumbent on me to clarify that what happens next is by no means a recommended remedy today. What standards were practiced in the Old Testament are very different from what today's laws and judgments demand in our civilized society. However, the basic principle has a timeless meaning. Throughout all of the Judeo-Christian teachings is a woven common thread of the necessity for the atonement of sin. We find in verse 14 of 2 Samuel that once certain members of Saul's family were condemned to die, since Saul was already dead, the curse was lifted, and the land was healed.

It is certainly noteworthy that David was a king when he inquired about the famine and when he made amends for Saul's breaking of the covenant against the Gibeonites. We find throughout the Scripture that the king is anointed by God. This means they enjoy special blessings and favor, but likewise, they have significantly more responsibility and accountability. And just as David refused to raise a hand against Saul when Saul was still a king, even though Saul was trying to kill David (1 Samuel 24:6), so we also must be mindful of how we act toward or even speak about our leaders, whether they're worthy of the position or not. While they are "anointed," there is a mantle over them that means God will protect them *if* they obey His laws and commands but will also punish them if they deserve it.

Whenever we try to overstep the boundary God has established, we are in danger of becoming partly responsible for the "curse," just like the leader who has broken the covenant in the first place. Therefore, it will take our president to initiate and lead the ultimate repentance and return to the LORD on behalf of our nation. That's why when Ronald Reagan was president, it was such a blessing to our land when he would speak about the need for spiritual renewal and how God wanted the United States to be that "shining city on a hill."

Puritan pilgrim John Winthrop, in perhaps the earliest example of the idea of American exceptionalism, in 1630, while still aboard a ship bound for Massachusetts Bay, delivered his sermon "A Model of Christian Charity."

> For we must consider that we shall be as a city upon a hill. The eyes of all people are upon us. So that if we shall deal falsely with our God in this work we have undertaken, and so cause Him to withdraw His present help from us, we shall be made a story and a by-word through the world.

In other words, become cursed. Winthrop also said, "We have another goal, another end. *We have entered into an explicit covenant with God to be His people in this New World.*" The pilgrims who came to the new world in 1607 incorporated within their Virginia compact the following statement:

> To propagate, to expand the gospel, the kingdom of the Lord Jesus Christ, and to take the gospel to people who were lying in darkness and had no knowledge of the one true God.

Citing our Declaration of Independence,

> We, therefore, the Representatives of the United States of America, in General Congress, Assembled, *appealing to the Supreme Judge of the world* for the rectitude of our intentions, and for the support of this Declaration, *with a firm reliance on the protection of Divine Providence*, we mutually pledge to each other our Lives, our Fortunes and our sacred Honor.

It was clearly understood and agreed upon in this timeless binding document of independence that our nation was founded on dependence on the Almighty Creator. Tearing down statues of these giants from our country's history will never undo this foundation. Expelling God's Word and prayer from our schools cannot erase the promise the framers of the Declaration of Independence and Constitution made to God. Even abandoning the Constitution, God forbid, could never repeal the covenant our nation is obligated to keep. Therefore, I say to all those who would seek to destroy the very spiritual framework and foundation of this land, please find yourselves somewhere else to live. In the immortal words of Merle Haggard, "If you don't love it, leave it!" ("The Fightin' Side of Me").

Since history is replete with similar accounts, in the following chapters, we will look at several others proving how seriously God takes covenant promises we make with Him and with others in His sight. All in all, the Bible lists over seven thousand promises from God. Here are some examples of what the Bible has to say about promises.

In Ecclesiastes 5:2 (NIV),

> Do not be quick with your mouth, do not be hasty in your heart to utter anything before God.

In Hebrews 10:23 (CSB),

> Let us hold on to the confession of our hope without wavering, since He who promised is faithful.

In Hebrews 6:13 (NIV),

> When God made His promise to Abraham, since there was no one greater for Him to swear by, He swore by Himself.

In 2 Corinthians 1:20 (CSB),

> For every one of God's promises is "Yes" in Him. Therefore, through Him we also say "Amen" to the glory of God.

In Joshua 21:45 (NIV),

> Not one of all the Lord's good promises to Israel failed, everyone was fulfilled.

In Isaiah 55:11 (NIV),

> Thus sayeth the Lord, "So it is with my word that goes out from my mouth: It will not return to me empty or void but will accomplish what I desire and achieve the purpose for which I sent."

Suffice to say, God's faithfulness and His desire for us to remain faithful are commensurate indeed. One doesn't have to study history much to learn that almost all the Founding Fathers were men of strong faith. They held fast to Judeo-Christian values that are now today in dire jeopardy of being abandoned. Certainly already, one is persecuted or "canceled" for making a stand on behalf of these ancient tenets. But our Founding Fathers knew that these core beliefs and values were from the very heart of God. They are how society ensures justice, law and order, and liberty for all.

For example, George Washington's famous prayer goes like this in part,

> Almighty God: We make our earnest prayer that Thou wilt keep the United States in Thy holy protection; that Thou wilt incline the hearts of the citizens to cultivate a spirit of subordination and obedience to government and entertain a brotherly affection and love for one another and for their fellow-citizens.

This was how our first president prayed to God. I wonder how our current one prays.

Thomas Jefferson said,

> God who gave us life gave us liberty. Can the liberties of a nation be secure when we have removed a conviction that these liberties are the gift of God? Indeed, I tremble for my country when I reflect that God is just, and that His justice cannot sleep forever.

In the *Diary and Autobiography of John Adams,*

> Suppose a nation in some distant region should take the Bible for their only law Book, and every member should regulate his conduct by the precepts there exhibited! Every member would be obliged in conscience, to temperance, frugality, and industry; to justice, kindness, and charity towards his fellow men; and to piety, love, and reverence toward Almighty God... What a Eutopia, what a Paradise would this region be.

In *The Trumpet Voice of Freedom: Patrick Henry of Virginia,*

> It cannot be emphasized too strongly or too often that this great nation was founded, not by religionists, but by Christians, not on religions, but on the gospel of Jesus Christ. For this very reason peoples of other faiths have been afforded asylum, prosperity, and freedom of worship here.

Benjamin Franklin said,

> Here is my Creed. I believe in one God, the Creator of the Universe. That He governs by His Providence. That He ought to be worshipped.

Abraham Lincoln was quoted as saying,

> The purposes of the Almighty are perfect, and must prevail, though we erring mortals may fail to accurately perceive them in advance.

And let's not forget which president was credited for establishing our country's motto, "In God we trust," and for inserting officially the words "under God" in our Pledge of Allegiance. Both of which are thanks to General Dwight David Eisenhower.

And I would be amiss if I didn't refer to at least some of my favorite president's quotes concerning faith in God.

> The time has come to turn to God and reassert our trust in Him for the healing of America— our country is in need of and ready for a spiritual renewal. (Ronald Reagan)

And his most famous one,

> If we ever forget that we're one nation
> under God, then we will be a nation gone under.
> (Ronald Reagan)

These were men of deep abiding faith and reliance in our Creator for all the blessings and liberty we enjoy and have enjoyed. Men who understood the cost of sacrifice for the greater good of the nation and its dream. A dream that was birthed in the heart of the Almighty, forged in the fire of war, and realized in fruition through the price of the ultimate sacrifice. However, there is no guarantee we will continue to enjoy the countless blessings of this dream known as liberty if our nation doesn't heed this warning. Repent and, in humility, seek God before it's too late. For as in every aspect of life, there are always conditions and consequences.

Chapter 2

Covenant Conditions and Consequences

Extremely pernicious is the mindset that says, "I tried my best, but after all, I have the right to change my mind." Too often we find in our society this ubiquitous attitude of complacency. That is exacerbated by the victim entitlement ideology, which is so pervasive, and it's no wonder we see more and more the degradation of our core family structure and multitudes of children being raised without a father, mother, or perhaps both. We must start to recognize this crisis and boldly declare this warning cry to everyone within our God-given sphere of influence. We must be sedulous in educating our next generation of the countless blessings we as a nation have enjoyed due to the divine protection and favor lavished on us from our Creator. And in turn, we must admonish them of the tenuous nature of that provision, which is predicated upon the covenant, made by our Founding Fathers with God, being understood, respected, and upheld. One of my favorite quotes from President Ronald Reagan is, "Freedom is never more than one generation away from becoming extinct."

The Scripture is full of verse after verse of conditions that God has placed on His promises. Second Chronicles 7:14 is arguably the best example: "If my people, who are called by my name, will humble themselves and pray and seek my face and turn from their wicked ways, then I will hear from heaven, and I will forgive their sin and will heal their land." The emphasis is on the first word, "If."

Certainly, God could simply choose to heal our land without our acknowledgment and repentance of our sins. However, because of the free will He has created all of mankind with, His divine order requires a partnership between man and God. Just as parents, we could simply choose to ignore our kids' mistakes or rebellions and still lavish them with gifts and special privileges; we would, however, be doing them a grave disservice by being so indulgent. Instead, we should give them one of the greatest gifts by placing conditions on the reward. This, in turn, teaches them the value of making the right decisions and exercising good judgment and responsibility.

Another great reminder to us of this principle of conditions is Psalm 91. Verses 9–10 state, "If I make the Most High my dwelling, even the LORD my refuge, then no harm will befall me, no disaster will come near my tent." Do you see it? The words *if* and *then* make it very clear and are most definitely not nugatory. There are certain God-ordained conditions to the blessings we enjoy. Now one could stop reading this book at this point and either throw it away or leave it to collect dust on a shelf. But that still doesn't negate the truth of this principle.

Whether we like it or not, this is the way God has created and established life to be. The good news is that with this conditional arrangement comes great certainty. A certainty God has guaranteed we can count on. A verse that exemplifies this beautifully is Psalm 91:14, "Because he loves me, declares the LORD, I will rescue him. I will protect him for he acknowledges my name." It goes on to say in verses 15–16, "He will call upon me and I will answer him. I will be with him in trouble. I will deliver him and honor him. With long life will I satisfy him and show him my salvation."

I believe the conditions that God has established are for our ultimate protection and good. Although when we deliberately choose to ignore them and rebel against His kingdom authority, we not only find danger but are also met with confusion. One sobering example of this is in the book of Joshua, chapter 7, "Achan pillaged an ingot of gold and a quantity of silver from Jericho, in contravention of Joshua's directive that 'all the silver, and gold, and vessels of brass and iron, are consecrated unto the Lord.'"

This one rapacious act of disobedience resulted in the Israelites being routed at Ai, defeated by a smaller and weaker group of people. The reason is that God wasn't standing with them at that point because the covenant was broken. Again, like with the Gibeonites, the remedy for this broken promise was severe and costly. And as another result, the Bible says Joshua was confused and uncertain about their purpose and calling.

Joshua said,

> LORD why did you ever bring this people across the Jordan to deliver us into the hands of the Amorites to destroy us? If only we had been content to stay on the other side of the Jordan! Pardon your servant, LORD. What can I say, now that Israel has been routed by its enemies? The Canaanites and the other people of the country will hear about this and they will surround us and wipe out our name from the earth. (Joshua 7:7–9)

One example of another country's demise is the former Empire of Russia (prior to the USSR) and, consequently, the former USSR also. Albeit less cataclysmic than the decimation of the former city of Jericho (circa 1,400 BC), the former Empire of Russia endured the Bloody Sunday massacre, which sparked the Russian Revolution of 1905, during which angry workers responded with a series of crippling strikes throughout the country.

Farm laborers and soldiers joined the cause, leading to the creation of worker-dominated councils called "soviets." In one incident, the crew of the battleship *Potemkin* staged a successful mutiny against their overbearing officers. Historians would later refer to the 1905 Russian Revolution as the "Great Dress Rehearsal," as it set the stage for the upheavals to come, such as when the empire succumbed to its destructive fate when the Bolsheviks led a rebellion starting in 1917, culminating in 1923 with the establishment of the USSR.

Interestingly, a century earlier in 1815, the Empire of Russia had formed a "Holy Alliance" with Austria and Prussia (Germany). Originally, this alliance (covenant) was formed in an attempt to restrain liberalism and secularism in Europe in the wake of the devastating French Revolutionary Wars and the Napoleonic Wars. The monarchs of the three expressions of Christian faith—Catholic (Austria), Protestant (Prussia), and Orthodox (Russia)—promised to act on the basis of "justice, love, and peace," both in internal and foreign affairs for "consolidating human institutions and remedying their imperfections."

Later reinstated in 1871, although its foundational goal was admirable to instill Christian values in European political life, after little more than a decade, the alliance began to falter and eventually dissolved over internal disputes concerning the dissolution of the Ottoman Empire. Once again, we find greed and self-centeredness being the precipitating motive that leads to the covenant being broken, which in turn weakened the Empire of Russia. Then severe famine during 1920–1922, a reoccurring curse on the land there not being dealt with appropriately, led to the empire's ultimate demise.

Of course, once the USSR took control and instituted the Communist mandate of national atheism, this inevitably led to that form of government's undoing as well. Ronald Reagan was credited as challenging General Secretary Gorbachev of the USSR by asking, "What if you ruled that religious freedom was part of the people's rights, that people of any religion could go to the church of their choice?" Reagan went on to say that if Gorbachev would guarantee religious tolerance, attitudes in America toward the Soviet Union would change dramatically. "You will be a hero, and much of the feeling against your country will disappear like water in hot sun."

We see today in our country hosts of good people discouraged, confused, and without hope. This is largely due to the fact that we, as a nation, have broken the covenant with God. Every time our school boards have banned prayer in schools, every time one of our courthouses or other government buildings have removed the Ten Commandments from display, and every time we have heard one of our nation's leaders purposely leave out the words *under God* when reciting the Pledge of Allegiance, we have sent a message to God Almighty that what the framers of our Constitution said and vowed doesn't matter. And we wonder why our cities' streets are running with blood, mass looting is occurring, folks don't know which pronoun or bathroom to use, and other countries see us as a weak and compromised nation. Then adding insult to injury, some of our nation's leaders still refuse to acknowledge our condition and sin.

A new study shows that America's Christian majority has been shrinking for years, and if recent trends continue, Christians could make up less than half the US population within a few decades (September 17, 2022, report). I believe this is a direct result of our nation's leaders not admitting the problem at hand nor leading the charge in reaffirming our commitment to the almost 250-year-old covenant.

One of the traits I most admire about the Orthodox Christian and Jewish faiths is their unyielding devotion to tradition and covenant with God. Regardless of current affairs, modern technology, distractions that would compete for their attention and time, they are steadfast to the ancient and sanctified ways. You can attend one of their services and swear you had stepped back in time through the centuries. It is truly a beautiful tribute to what the LORD has established for His people regarding worship.

Now I am not saying that the newer styles of worship services one can attend at a more modern church or synagogue are necessarily inferior—not at all. I thank the LORD there are various streams within the headwaters of faith in the living God. Obviously, mine is with the Christian faith; however, I firmly believe that any Christian who claims to love the LORD with all their heart, soul, and strength had better also love and feel a divine connection to a person of the Jewish faith. After all, they are "God's chosen people." To say one loves God but then doesn't defend and support Israel means that person is being somewhat disingenuous.

Lying about it only makes matters worse, as in the case of Ananias and Sapphira in Acts 5 of the Bible. Here, a man and his wife deliberately plotted to hold back a portion of the money, in secret, when they sold some land and then lied to the apostles about the amount they made from the sale. The result of this was the sudden demise of both guilty parties. Here, the lie was the greater sin since a covenant agreement had been made among the believers that they would share with one another as they had means. After all, one of the seven deadly sins God hates is a lying tongue (*Proverbs 6:16–17*). Another powerful reminder of this is found in Proverbs 29:18, "Where there is no vision [*revelation/truth*], the people perish [*cast off restraint*]. But blessed is he who keeps the law [*covenant*]" (*italics—other translations*).

In the end, it's undeniably evident that a lack of conditions leads to a lack of constraint; then in turn, the covenant is abandoned, which always leads to the death of something—death of a marriage, death of a value system, or even death of the dream this great nation was founded on. We mustn't allow that to happen. We must pray.

Chapter 3

Covenant Prayer

Joel 2:13 tells us to "rend your heart and not your garments. Return to the LORD your God, for He is gracious and compassionate, slow to anger and abounding in love, and He relents from sending calamity."

Second Chronicles 7:14, as mentioned previously, is one of the most famously quoted verses for how God wants His people to pray in humility and repentance.

Isaiah 58:1–14 depicts for us how to (and how not to) truly fast and pray,

> Is this not the fast that I have chosen sayeth the LORD: To loose the bonds of wickedness, to undo the heavy burdens, to let the oppressed go free, and that you break every yoke? Is it not to share your bread with the hungry, and that you bring to your house the poor who are cast out; when you see the naked, that you cover him, and not hide yourself from your own flesh? Then your light shall break forth like the morning, your healing shall spring forth speedily, and your righteousness shall go before you; the glory of the LORD shall be your rear guard. Then you shall call, and the LORD will answer; you shall cry, and

He will say, "Here I am." If you take away the yoke from your midst, the pointing of the finger, and speaking wickedness; if you extend your soul to the hungry and satisfy the afflicted soul, then your light shall dawn in the darkness, and your darkness shall be as the noonday. The LORD will guide you continually, and satisfy your soul in drought, and strengthen your bones. You shall be like a watered garden, and like a spring of water, whose waters do not fail. Those from among you shall build up the old ruins. You shall raise up the foundations of many generations; and you shall be called Repairer of the breach *[broken covenant]*, the Restorer of streets to dwell in.

We must pray for unity within the church, as well as peace within our nation, if this is to be our reality. We must also pray for and support Israel if we want to see our nation truly healed and restored, enjoying God's ultimate blessing (*Genesis 12:1–3, Abrahamic Covenant*).

"The time has come to turn to God and reassert our trust in Him for the healing of America—our country is in need of and ready for a spiritual renewal" (Ronald Reagan).

I believe the former president was speaking of a humble and contrite confession because of breaking the covenant with God and acknowledging our utter dependence on the Almighty and our collective culpability for the state of our nation. There is a biblical principle known as "identification repentance." Another translation is "standing in the gap." Referring to the Messiah in Isaiah 53:12, "Because He poured out His life unto death and was *numbered with the transgressors*. For He bore the sin of many and made intercession for the transgressors." In Ezekiel 22:30, "I looked for someone among them who would build up the wall and *stand before me in the gap* on behalf of the land so I would not have to destroy it."

James 4:8 instructs us to "draw near to God and He will draw near to us." When I was growing up as a young boy, there used to be a saying in the church my family attended—"travailing prayer."

Basically, this is what David meant when he wrote Psalm 5:2, "Give heed to the voice of my cry, my King and my God, for to You I will pray" *(without ceasing—from 1 Thessalonians 5:17)*.

And in Psalm 84:2, "My soul yearns, even faints, for the courts of the LORD; my heart and my flesh cry out for the living God." "It is only when the whole heart is gripped with the passion of prayer that the life-giving fire descends, for none but the earnest man gets access to the ear of God" (E. M. Bounds).

Regarding prayer for those in leadership over our nation, the Bible is very clear what our posture should be:

> Therefore, I exhort first of all that supplications, prayers, intercessions, and giving of thanks be made for all men, for kings and all who are in authority, that we may lead a quiet and peaceable life in all godliness and reverence. For this is good and acceptable in the sight of God our Savior, who desires all men to be saved and to come to the knowledge of the truth. (1 Timothy 2:1–3)

Also, we are admonished in Romans 13:1–2,

> Let every person be subordinate to the higher authorities, for there is no authority except from God, and those that exist have been established by God. Therefore, whoever resists authority opposes what God has appointed, and those who do will bring judgment on themselves.

When was the last time we prayed for a president we didn't vote for?

Lord knows I have been just as guilty as the next person for not pressing through with the necessary number of hours of relentless prayer that it takes sometimes to see a breakthrough. Perhaps we ought to ask ourselves that question the next time we complain about the election results. We must, as God's people, make prayer a higher priority—higher than watching television or using social media or any other hobby or interest that could become an idol if left unchecked. I am not saying those other things are necessarily wrong or harmful; it's just that anything we allow to take first place in our lives, other than God, can become the very obstacle to seeing God's will accomplished on earth.

There is a powerful aspect of prayer where we actually come into agreement with God. As mentioned in the previous chapter, God in His sovereignty invites us, as His people, to partner with Him. What an amazing concept! But just as ineffective as a business would be, if both partners couldn't agree on strategy and policy, so also our nation is ineffective in fulfilling its God-given purpose due to a lack of agreement with God—and each other.

Pastor Jack Hayford once said, "Prayer is essentially a partnership of the redeemed child of God working hand in hand with God toward the realization of His redemptive purposes on earth." I believe this is a principle that is oftentimes hard to accept, let alone embrace. The reason is that it requires a surrender of our own selfish agenda and will. To merely say God is the LORD of our lives and then actually prove it by our actions are two different propositions.

James 5:16–18 says,

> Therefore confess your sins to each other and pray for each other so that you may be healed. The prayer of a righteous person is powerful and effective.
>
> Elijah was a human being, even as we are. He prayed earnestly that it would not rain, and it did not rain on the land for three and a half years. Again, he prayed, and the heavens gave rain, and the earth produced its crops.

Interesting to note is that prior to those encouraging words, we find this rebuke earlier in the same chapter,

> Now listen, you rich people, weep and wail because of the misery that is coming on you. Your

wealth has rotted, and moths have eaten your clothes. Your gold and silver are corroded. You have hoarded wealth in the last days. Look! The wages you failed to pay the workers who mowed your fields are crying out against you. The cries of the harvesters have reached the ears of the Lord Almighty. You have lived on earth in luxury and self-indulgence. You have fattened yourselves in the day of slaughter. You have condemned and murdered the innocent one, who was not opposing you.

Does that sound familiar today?

Good thing I am a firm believer in hope, especially the hope we have in the Lord God. Romans 15:13 says, "May the God of hope fill you with all joy and peace as you trust in Him, so that you may overflow with hope through the power of the Holy Spirit." These are very encouraging words! And I believe there's still hope for our nation. Being all gloom and doom won't turn the tide in the right direction. We need to speak life into the situation we're facing as a nation.

Proverbs 18:21 tells us, "The power of life and death is in the spoken word." We hear enough negativity on the news. We hear enough gaslighting and accusatory rhetoric from each side of the aisle. What we need are words of truth and hope being spoken at our kitchen tables, in our schools, in our churches and synagogues, and yes, in every branch of government. John 8:32 reminds us, "We shall know the truth and the truth shall set us free." Once we hear the truth, God's truth, proclaimed everywhere from the White House to the remote farmhouse, then we will see our country set free from the chains of hatred, bitterness, and greed.

A powerful account of hope from our nation's history is the story of the miracle at the Old South Church in Massachusetts. In October 1746, prior to the French and Indian War, during what came to be known as King George's War, France had sent a large fleet of almost one hundred ships to attack the colonies and burn those coastal cities of America. The colonists had no chance of defending, let alone staging, any counteroffensive. The governor of Massachusetts assembled a day of prayer and fasting, urging all citizens to beseech the Almighty for divine intervention.

As the French fleet was rapidly approaching the coastline, the Reverend Thomas Prince at the Old South Church began to pray, "Deliver us from our enemy! Send Thy tempest, Lord, upon the waters to the eastward. Raise Thy hand and scatter the ships of our tormentors and drive them hence. Sink their proud frigates beneath the power of Thy mighty winds!" He had scarcely finished the prayer when the sun was consumed by darkness, and there rose a great tempest in the ocean. At hearing the shutters and windows of the old church shake and the church bell ringing erratically, Rev. Prince raised his hands and prayed, "We hear Thy voice, Lord! Thy bell tolls for the death of our enemies. Thine be the glory, Lord. Amen!" The following week, the colonists learned a miracle had occurred. A virtual hurricane had risen in the North Atlantic and sunk nearly all the French ships. The remaining ones returned to France broken and battered. God had protected and defended His people who called upon His name.

One of my favorite stories from WWII is "Patton's Prayer." Actually, it was General Patton's chaplain who wrote the prayer. Patton ordered his chaplain to compose a powerful prayer that would implore God to move on the Third Army's behalf and provide more conducive weather to aid them in battle. Getting to Bastogne in time to rescue the 101st Airborne Division from the German Army was of paramount consequence. If Patton's Third Army had not made it on time because of bad weather, the Germans may have broken through and made it to the port city of Antwerp, where they would have received fresh supplies and possibly been able to prolong the European theater of the war.

God answered Patton's prayer, the weather cleared, and the famed Third Army arrived just in time to repel the German Army and eventually advance into Berlin to defeat the Nazis, leading ultimately to VE (Victory in Europe) Day. The prayer went as follows:

Almighty and most merciful Father, we
humbly beseech Thee, of Thy great goodness,

to restrain these immoderate rains with which have had to contend. Grant us fair weather for Battle. Graciously hearken to us as soldiers who call upon Thee that, armed with Thy power, we may advance from victory to victory, and crush the oppression of wickedness of our enemies and establish Thy justice among men and nations.

We find a perfect example of the proper attitude our legislators today should all adopt. At the age of eighty-one, Benjamin Franklin uttered his famous speech during the Constitutional Convention:

The small progress we have made after 4 or 5 weeks of close attendance & continual reasonings with each other, our different sentiments on almost every question, several of the last producing as many noes as ays, is methinks a melancholy proof of the imperfection of the human understanding. We indeed seem to feel our own want of political wisdom, since we have been running about in search of it. We have gone back to ancient history for models of government and examined the different forms of those Republics which having been formed with the seeds of their own dissolution now no longer exist. And we have viewed modern States all round Europe but find none of their Constitutions suitable to our circumstances.

In this situation of this Assembly groping as it were in the dark to find political truth, and scarce able to distinguish it when presented to us, how has it happened, Sir, that we have not hitherto once thought of humbly applying to the Father of lights to illuminate our understandings? In the beginning of the contest with Great Britain, when we were sensible of danger we had daily prayer in this room for the Divine Protection. Our prayers, Sir, were heard, and they were graciously answered. All of us who were engaged in the struggle must have observed frequent instances of a Superintending Providence in our favor. To that kind providence we owe this happy opportunity of consulting in peace on the means of establishing our future national felicity. And have we now forgotten that powerful Friend? Or do we imagine that we no longer need His assistance. I have lived, Sir, a long time and the longer I live, the more convincing proofs I see of this truth that God governs in the affairs of men. And if a sparrow cannot fall to the ground without His notice, is it probable that an empire can rise without His aid? We have been assured, Sir, in the sacred writings that "except the Lord build, they labor in vain that build it." I firmly believe this; and I also believe that without His concurring aid we shall succeed in this political building no better than the Builders of Babel. We shall be divided by our little partial local interests; our projects will be confounded, and we ourselves shall be become a reproach and a bye word down to future age. And what is worse, mankind may hereafter from this unfortunate instance, despair of establishing governments by human wisdom, and leave it to chance, war, and conquest. I therefore beg leave to move—that henceforth prayers imploring the assistance of Heaven, and its blessings on our deliberations, be held in this Assembly every morning before we proceed to business.

These are inspired words and sound advice for us to follow if we are to ever see the reconciliation and restoration of the covenant.

Chapter 4

Covenant Reconciliation
and Restoration

> "Even now," declares the LORD, "return to
> me with all your heart, with fasting and weeping
> and mourning. I will restore to you the years the
> locusts have eaten [*meaning the years that were
> lost*]." (Joel 2:12 and 25)

God loves to make restorations for things that were once thought to be lost forever and destroyed. No matter what the situation, our God is in the business of breathing back to life what we may have caused to die because of our disobedience or lack of faithfulness. Just as a marriage on the brink of divorce can be saved by one touch of the Master's hand, so, also, our nation can still be restored to what the Founding Fathers envisioned. A land where everyone has the God-given right to enjoy liberty and pursue happiness, where the outcome of feeling fulfilled is merely dependent upon each person's willingness to apply the principles of hard work and sacrifice, graced with courage from our Creator.

Second Corinthians 5:18 tells us, "And all of this is a gift from God, who *reconciled* us back to Himself through Christ. And God has given us *the ministry of reconciliation*." We need to understand that because of the partnering God desires from us, the goal of reconciling what is broken is entrusted to us as His people. Therefore, if we are to realize the goal of reconciling our nation back to God, it will depend on us to do the heavy lifting.

I realize many among us are content to go on being complacent or, at best, naive. They would insist the status quo is just fine. However, anyone who has experienced either directly or indirectly the frustration and even pain of watching a person standing quietly on a street corner get hit in the head by a thug with a sucker punch knows it's time for a change in our country! We are, as a nation, more divided now than I have ever seen in my lifetime. Our polarized beliefs and convictions have created this chasm between us filled with toxic animosity.

Before we get too far into how the covenant is restored and how we can then be reconciled to God, as a nation, allow me to share a few suggestions for preventive measures we can take to ensure our situation doesn't worsen. First, I believe that until our public school systems are transformed back to where they used to be in the '50s, for example, the best parents can do is either homeschool their kids or use worthy private schools for education. Next, find a solid church or synagogue to attend and be involved with where the truth is declared boldly and unashamedly. Too many of our religious institutions today have become spineless and scared. They are scared of being perceived as "political," too conservative, or, even worse, controversial. Lastly, we must be on the offensive. Stand firm in your convictions and share your beliefs with others regardless of political party affiliation.

Too many on the other side of the aisle refuse to speak with a conservative or liberal. That's unfortunate since discourse is essential if things are ever to change. Just make sure you share your convictions with compassion and humility. Remember the words of the apostle Paul,

> A servant of the Lord must not quarrel but be gentle to all, patient, able to teach, in humility correcting those who are in opposition. If God perhaps will grant them repentance so they may know the truth and escape the snare of the devil. (2 Timothy 2:24–26 NKJV)

I realize we conservatives like to think that God is a Republican, but I must break the news—He is not. God is neither Republican nor Democrat. He is the One True Living God! And He deserves our devotion, worship, and surrender. If we, as a nation, are ever to see true healing, reconciliation, and restoration, we will have to first get past the political rhetoric. We must stop seeing the other side as the enemy and instead recognize there is a real enemy of all people's souls.

The Bible tells us that Satan's main mission is to steal, kill, and destroy (John 10:10). I hate to say it, but we're letting him do a pretty good job in our country recently. Let's stop spending all our energy on defeating one another and instead focus on taking any cultural hegemony away from this demonic agent of death.

To restore our nation's covenant with God, we will have to be in agreement—just as our Founding Fathers were when those awesome and inspired documents were written and dedicated to the Almighty. It will also take showing God how much we want the restoration and healing of our nation to occur. A great example of this principle is found in Mark 7.

> A woman who was a Greek, a Syro-Phoenician by birth, kept asking Jesus to cast the demon out of her daughter. But Jesus said to her, "Let the children be filled first, for it is not good to take the children's bread and throw it to the little dogs." And she answered and said to Him, "Yes, Lord, yet even the little dogs under the table eat from the children's crumbs." Then He said to her, "For this response go your way; the demon has gone out of your daughter." And when she had come to her house, she found the demon had indeed left her daughter.

I think if it had been most of us, we might have been inclined to walk away feeling rejected or offended but then would have missed out on the miracle—the healing. God simply wants us to demonstrate with our actions, as well as words, how committed and earnest we are.

I feel strongly that the LORD is asking us as a nation, "Do you want to be healed?" It is just like He did with the man who was crippled and sat by the pool full of healing waters every day yet couldn't get in the water (John 5). Truly wanting healing implies being willing to do the work of rehabilitation in whatever form is required. This "rehabilitation" could take on many different forms in our society, such as going out of our way to sit with a person from the other side of the political aisle and calmly listening to their opinion without spewing anger and disdain in some judgmental diatribe. Another form might be showing support for a local politician that perhaps we didn't vote for by participating in one of their charitable community fundraising events. Or maybe we simply need to say a sincere prayer to the Almighty on behalf of our president, asking for wisdom and discernment to be bestowed.

Regardless of what the action might look like, the concept is universal—get outside of our comfort zones and reach out with the hand of brotherly kindness. After all, we must remember, "Every kingdom divided against itself is laid waste, and a divided household falls" (Luke 11:17). The Bible also instructs us in Romans 12:10, "Be devoted to one another in love. Honor one another above yourselves."

We will inevitably face rejection and even persecution as we take this bold step. However, we must persist, even if at the end of the day all we can accomplish is our own changed heart and mind toward others. The apostle Paul wrote, "As much as it depends on you, live at peace with everyone" (Romans 12:18).

One of the most renowned and admirable traits of Abraham Lincoln was his innate ability to bring people together despite their differences. Let's not forget that without President Lincoln's passion for preserving our Union, the Thirteenth, Fourteenth, and Fifteenth Amendments to the Constitution would not have been ratified until much later, two of which were posthumously for Lincoln.

It is certainly interesting and ironic that part of what it took to ultimately preserve the Union was war, a bloody and devastating Civil War. The ultimate outcome made the costly sacrifice worthy— the end of slavery in our country!

Yet as abhorrent a sin as slavery was, it is also extremely disturbing to watch how the pendulum has swung to the extreme opposite end in the last few years and even full circle today, with this CRT and "white-shame" ideology. This form of racism is detestable also, as is what happened in our nation's earlier years up through to the Civil Rights Movement. These egregious mindsets of bigotry break the very heart of God and lead only to division and hatred.

Back to Lincoln. It was honest Abe who first proclaimed publicly as a sitting president of the United States that racism had to end. That it was not God's will for His people. And that we, as a whole nation, were called and created to be free. The Great Emancipator once said, "Those who deny freedom to others, deserve it not for themselves; and, under a just God, cannot long retain it." It was his unwavering dedication to abolishing that sinful stain of slavery that had plagued our country that led to a nation being reconciled and restored by the grace of God.

Not many realize that this president's views in the last few years of his life were somewhat different from the position Lincoln had held several years earlier in Charleston, Illinois, when he was debating senate incumbent and political rival, Stephen A. Douglas. The point is that a legend from our country's hall of fame, and one of the greatest presidents we've had, overcame an upbringing and societal indoctrination over many years to change into a person of deep conviction regarding the God-given freedom all God's children deserve. That kind of metamorphosis could only occur in a free society where people actually were allowed and encouraged to have challenging ideas and engaging discourse with civility and mutual respect. Unfortunately, that is not the society we are seeing evolve before our eyes today, where people are fired from their jobs, canceled on social media, or even ostracized from their families if they dare convey a contrary view.

When looking further at Abraham Lincoln's example, we see the steps he took to promote, and ultimately achieve, reunifying our nation together as one Union, were as follows:

- Implementing the "Proclamation of Amnesty and Reconstruction," which was contingent upon the person(s) tak-

ing an oath of loyalty to the Union and accepting the abo-
lition of slavery.

- Signing into effect the "Emancipation Proclamation" when he was quoted saying, *I never in my life felt more certain that I was doing right than I do in signing this paper.*
- Implementing policies aimed at "sectional reconciliation," which specifically brought certain southern states back into the Union even prior to the end of the Civil War and resulted in the abolishment of slavery in those states.

These are just to name a few. The question you may have is, What does this have to do with a covenant with God? Well, our nation had already broken the covenant with God when we allowed the first slave to be sold on our land. Since we know, of course, this was an act of sinful disobedience to the laws of God, what Lincoln did and others like him was paramount to restoring the covenant.

James Buchanan, arguably the worst president our nation has had, gives us a haunting picture of what not to do if you want to heal and restore a divided country. He was certainly two-faced, placating the abolitionists by feigning antislavery sentiments—all the while really supporting the proslavery Southern states.

Regarding his secretary of war, "Floyd even purposely scattered the Army so that much of it could be captured when hostilities should commence (*at the onset of the Civil War*), and distributed the cannon and small arms from Northern arsenals throughout the South so as to be on hand when treason wanted them" (*Ulysses S. Grant wrote in his memoirs*). Floyd eventually resigned and became a Confederate general. This sends a resounding message that deceitfulness and hypocrisy always lead to pain and suffering. Buchanan's duplicity led to Abraham Lincoln inheriting seven states that seceded from the Union by the time Lincoln was inaugurated in March of 1861.

I believe some of the basic foundational precepts that all of us older than forty-five years of age were taught are hardly being instilled in the younger generations anymore. These would include expressing gratitude, respecting one another, saying sorry and accepting responsibility for one's mistakes, telling the truth always, and working hard

to earn raises and bonuses instead of feeling like they're entitled to them. Perhaps if we could start teaching these ancient principles of good behavior to the next generation, we will see a society reborn of men and women who embrace and understand the need to keep covenant and cherish our nation's history and learn from it.

Now I realize at this point in the book that there are most likely only two major types of readers remaining. Either the one who is sincerely aligned with this book's theme and motive or, the other, the naysayer who merely wants to mock the author as a closed-minded Bible-thumping old-fashioned religious zealot. To the latter, I would propose the following question: If you have children or, if not, perhaps a young niece or nephew or maybe a dear friend with little ones, what kind of America do you want them to inherit? A nation that espouses dignity and respect for all regardless of skin color or ancestry? A nation founded on "heavenly" principles such as unconditional love and forgiveness? A nation that understands its duty and responsibility to be that "Shining City on a Hill"? Or a nation left to the next generation that is nothing more than a chaotic, recalcitrant society, where anarchy and self-indulgence reign?

If you think I'm exaggerating, just watch the news on all the channels from both sides. Or better yet, take a walk down a big city street at night filled with stores being looted and cars being vandalized, and then let's talk.

Just as when one is restoring an old house, there are parts of that house that may need to be removed and destroyed because of their rotten conditions. Otherwise, the end result could be the spreading of the termites or mold, for instance, throughout the entire house. This is the "pruning" process that takes hard work and commitment to achieve the desired end goal—a fully restored house, or nation, that can be enjoyed and lived in with prosperity and vigor.

We must carry out the process of removing the dead portions with wisdom, discernment, and care. One example of this is the judicial system our nation has instituted since its conception. When a lawbreaker violates the rules of law and order in a civilized society, there must be consequences such as incarceration, which is a necessary removal from society. Also, regarding our judicial branch of government, I would be remiss if I didn't make mention of the rectifying act of overturning *Roe v. Wade* on June 24, 2022, by the US Supreme Court. The horrific atrocity of all the millions of unborn children killed throughout our nation's history is yet another example of the breaking of the covenant with our Creator. We must seek God's forgiveness as a nation for allowing this to happen in order to see true restoration and healing occur.

In the book of Nehemiah, we see a clear picture of what it looks like when someone is committed to restoring what was lost and broken. Nehemiah, whose name means "God comforts," was the governor of Persian Judea during the fifth century BC. This was one of Israel's periods of exile and captivity. Nehemiah was called by God to "stand in the gap" and rebuild the wall, which was part of the Second Temple period and the key to reestablishing the Jewish way of life and the covenant they had with God. The wall Nehemiah rebuilt had been destroyed when the Chaldeans (Babylonians) conquered the city of Jerusalem.

Despite overwhelming opposition and ridicule from his own people, Nehemiah was sedulous about completing the task the Lord had given him. The significance of the wall being restored was the symbol and, more importantly, the assurance of protection and belonging. Amazingly, Nehemiah and his people finished rebuilding the walls around Jerusalem in only fifty-two days. Another significance to Nehemiah being the one to first sense the call from God and, in obedience, go to Jerusalem to inspect the walls in ruin and consequently oversee the rebuilding was his position as a leader—governor of Israel at that time. As mentioned previously in this book, it will take our leaders to lead the way.

A powerful example of a nation's restoration is the State of Israel. Found in Exodus 19 and 24 is the covenant God establishes with the people of Israel at Mount Sinai after He led them out of Egyptian slavery (*the Mosaic Covenant*). With it, God supplies the Law that is meant to govern and shape the people of Israel in the promised land (Canaan). This took place approximately in the thirteenth century BC. Then fast-forward to 733 BC when Israel first went into captivity during the Assyrian exile, followed by the Babylonian captivity, in which portions of the population of the kingdom of Judah were deported in 597 BC and again in 586 BC by the Neo-Babylonian Empire under the rule of Nebuchadnezzar II.

Shortly after that period was the freeing by the Persian Empire in 539 BC. Then in AD 70, the Roman Army besieged Jerusalem, and following a brutal five-month siege, the Romans destroyed the city and the Second Jewish Temple, and the nation of Israel yet again experienced exile. Then came the heinous atrocities of the Holocaust that resulted in the mass genocide of millions of Jews. However, in the midst of centuries of upheaval and turmoil, pain, and suffering, the people of Israel continued to cling to their faith and way of life.

Ultimately, on May 14, 1948, the modern-day nation of Israel became the world's first Jewish state in two millennia. It represents for Jews the restoration of their homeland after the centuries-long diaspora. Here we find evidence of *hope in future reconciliation because of strong abiding faith, devotion, and upholding covenant—and eventually, restoration because of God's faithfulness and love, rewarding His people for their faithfulness.* Not to oversimplify this epic saga, but God is merely wanting His people to return to Him and honor Him with their lives and their hearts. Will we as Americans answer the call and respond in faithfulness?

Chapter 5

Covenant Purpose

In this day and age we live in, with contracts for everything from cellular phone service to cable TV carriers, we grow weary of the negative stigma that a binding contract carries with it. The days of a handshake being sufficient for a deal to be secured seem nostalgic yet long gone. In our highly litigious society, we find very little solace when a person says, "You have my word."

All too often, we forget the One whose word means life and liberty. He alone is the Creator of us all and the ultimate Creator of the perfect contract—the only true secure deal. The covenant we make with God Almighty is intended to provide "Shalom shalom," which is translated from the Hebrew meaning "perfect peace, wholeness, and tranquility." We all could use more of this today in a world saturated with selfish ambition and vindictive agendas. Yet we fail to perceive the obvious source of what we all are longing for innately, which is being whole and complete.

This source is a binding relationship with the living God—a covenant relationship. Only in such a relationship do we find a harmonious outcome in the midst of a chaotic world. Here, we find the ability to enter into abiding rest in the face of capricious influences—grace and wisdom in the absence of sanity and civility. We cannot expect to achieve this place of peace and wholeness unless we are willing to abandon certain ideologies that are fundamentally contrary to the truth of who God is and the principles upon which this great nation was founded. Otherwise, we will always be dealing with the fallout of disingenuous indoctrination, such as the "woke" religion we see invading our schools, permeating our workplaces and government, and transforming our military.

There is no place for falsehood when what we desperately need is a return to the truth of God's Word. This new *woke* ideology is solely based on an attempt to evoke feelings of self-righteousness and to placate certain groups that refuse to accept we have evolved as a nation and repented already of the sins of our past. Our Founding Fathers were certainly not perfect, and this book is not intended to paint any such picture. We have made many mistakes as a nation throughout centuries of growing pains, yet by and large, we have learned from those mistakes. Thank God.

We must remain vigilant and steadfast on the vision this country has cherished, fought, and bled for now for over four hundred years since the first colonists landed on our shores. Their vision was to be free, free to worship according to their conscience. This idea of personal liberty and religious freedom has been the stalwart anchor that has allowed us as a nation to weather many storms, obstacles, and enemies—both foreign and domestic.

One of the main purposes for establishing a covenant is to protect the vision—to ensure we stay focused on what matters most, our life's primary purposes. I say that not as a singular purpose but rather as multiple purposes, for I am convinced we all have more than one purpose God created us for. It is all too easy to get off track in this fast-paced world where so many distractions seduce us and compete for our devotion and even worship. Giving in to these distractions is the main killer of the vision God has for us. As mentioned earlier, the Bible warns us, "Where there is no vision the people perish." I believe this is referring to a perishing of the soul and spirit, as well as life itself. We all desperately need, at times, to regain a fresh glimpse of that dream that keeps us young at heart—the vision that gives us the energy and resolve to keep pushing forward. It's when we lose that dream entirely that lives become shattered by hopelessness and relationships become burdensome and abandoned. At that point, or hopefully before, we have the decision to make. Will we take on the victim role, or will we use the struggle as a catalyst for change and growth?

Regarding the victim mindset so widespread in our society today, I am not intending to pass judgment at all, but rather, I offer food for thought and prayerful consideration. Generational curses, such as poverty, racism, hatred, fear, alcoholism, and drug addiction, can create a self-fulfilling prophecy that keeps people from realizing their full potential and becoming everything God created them to be. When we see a homeless person on a street corner the next time, instead of entertaining some captious or condescending attitude, let's try remembering that their story could be the result of a certain lie or lies that they were raised believing. That person could be enslaved by chains that were fettered long before they were even born. It could be perhaps a negative confession or proclamation made by a parent or even after birth by someone in authority and influence over them who abused that position of trust. This perpetuating cycle creates a warped sense of dependence upon the broken things in the past. Things that are best left in the past are instead often carried around with us like a prisoner's ball and chain.

Patrick Henry's quote, "When people forget God, tyrants establish their chains," is so very true.

We must be set free from these chains of victimization to see the American dream fulfilled and our nation healed and restored to what God and our Founding Fathers envisioned. John 8:32 tells us, "You shall know truth and the truth shall set you free." We must earnestly keep speaking the truth, the truth of what God says, to help set others free.

There are so many in our country who have been enslaved by lies and generational curses, yet hearing a compassionate word of truth spoken over their lives with love could be all it takes to destroy the deceptive illusion, bring an end to the blaming cycle of their past, and tear down the walls of captivity. Speaking positive confessions and declarations over people can lead to a future full of liberty and joy that truly is indescribable.

My parents were very spiritual, godly people. They believed in this timeless principle of speaking reality into existence. When I was born, they named me David for the sole reason that I would be a man after God's own heart, like David was in the Bible. Now I certainly have had my failures and regrets. However, one thing that has always remained constant at the core of my life is the truth and reality of how God sees me. The compelling certainty of His unfailing love and faithful promises in my life have kept me going in some of life's darkest times.

When I was twenty-three years old, my parents were both killed in a car accident. This tragedy, which certainly took a toll on my life for several years, never destroyed my faith or vision of God's calling in my life—to be a worshiper and man after God's own heart! I am forever grateful for the covenant my parents made with God even before I was born. For it is this covenant, which was passed down from my parents to me and since to my son and now grandchildren, that ensures a legacy worth living for. The fact is, there are so many in our nation who need to inherit a new legacy. A legacy full of hope and confidence. A legacy full of joy and peace. A legacy that they can hand down to their descendants with gratefulness. It only takes starting with one. Ronald Reagan once said, "We can't help everyone, but everyone can help someone."

This was what our Founding Fathers understood and the reason they embraced such an eternal covenant with God. They knew the unchanging truth that only when we surrender to the One who wants the very best for our lives and cares more profoundly for us than we could ever care for ourselves do we truly find life with purpose and freedom. Otherwise, we are continually searching for the next self-gratifying crusade or ideology. Without realizing it, we succumb to the oldest of sins, pride. And in this place of arrogance and self-centered euphoria, albeit false euphoria, we begin to see ourselves as gods. This is the reason we see such a ubiquitous cascade of sanctimonious rhetoric in our society.

There are those who cannot fathom submitting to a higher authority—the Creator of the universe. They would rather trade divine protection and peace for a temporal fleeting illusion of moral high ground. In the end, the plethora of virtuous platitudes only serves to reinforce the reality that man is incapable of achieving any level of divinity. There is only One who is worthy of our praise, worship, and allegiance—our sovereign Creator.

This is the overwhelming reason we need to embrace and enter into a covenant agreement once again with the Almighty. This realization of our own humanity and imperfection is the impetus that compels us to submit to God's will and authority in our lives and ultimately for our nation—to humble ourselves before God, and as His Word promises, "He will lift us up" (*James 4:10*). Then and only then will we see our nation made whole and realize its true God-given purpose.

Hannah was such a person who needed God to lift her up. She was childless and in desperate need of a miracle. It was her heart's longing to have a son. So she humbled herself before the LORD, in the book of 1 Samuel, and made a promise to God, the Miracle Worker. The binding agreement was made, and when God answered her plea and granted her a child, her son, Samuel, was born. Living up to her part of the deal, as she had promised, once Samuel was only three years old, she took him to live in the temple of the LORD. There, Samuel would grow under the oversight of the priest Eli.

The Bible says, "The LORD was with Samuel as he grew up and let none of his words fall to the ground." When Samuel was twelve years old, the LORD began to speak to Samuel in an audible voice. Samuel's response, at the instruction of the priest, was simply, "Speak[,] LORD, for your servant is listening." In that one act of obedience, and as a result of the covenant Hannah made with God, Samuel became one of the greatest prophets in history. His purpose, in addition to anointing David as Israel's king, was to bring forth hope and a future for God's people.

Chapter 6

Covenant Future and Hope

In Jeremiah 29:11, the LORD promises, "For I know the plans I have for you…plans to give you hope and a future."

Proverbs 13:12 says, "Hope deferred makes the heart sick, but a longing fulfilled is a tree of life."

When thinking about the future of our great nation and where we need to be to ensure hope and prosperity for the next generations to come, it's interesting to examine the following comparison. Especially today, we hear a lot of talk about our democracy being in jeopardy. However, the same folks saying that must not either understand or want to admit that our country was never founded as a democracy but rather as a Constitutional Republic.

I would liken the two to either being in covenant agreement with God or a self-indulgent abdication of freedom. We can see clearly that the safeguards that ensure liberty and the individual's rights being truly preserved and protected are actually found only within the Constitutional Republic, which is the same as the covering we enjoy within the covenant our Founding Fathers made with God. The illusion of democracy being somehow a free state of existence is a great deception. The reason is that democracy, as Thomas Jefferson put it so accurately, "is nothing more than mob rule, where 51% of the people may take away the rights of the other 49%."

This—coupled with the fact that within a democracy, the ruler (the president, for example) is always under the temptation to usurp absolute control and power—is usually a relatively easy achievement given that the people have most likely already been convinced to capitulate their rights and let the government take over the decision-making and dictate what they can and cannot do or think. Just like with the sardonic quote of Ronald Reagan, "I'm with the government and we're here to help." Rather, it is when we submit to the Almighty and His laws that we find true freedom and liberty. God doesn't want us to be robots; otherwise, He wouldn't have given us free will. He wants us to enjoy freedom—freedom from the bondage of sin and harmful actions and freedom from their painful consequences, all of which are born out of self-centered thinking, fear, and pride.

Moving forward, if the country that we love, or at least should love, is to be truly healed and remain whole and committed to the covenant it was founded on, then we must destroy the root of hypocrisy so prevalent today. Throughout the Scripture, we find abundant evidence that God hates hypocrisy. In the book of Matthew, chapter 23, Jesus uses the word *hypocrites* six times when addressing the leaders of that day (Pharisees). I think the most relevant to today's condition is verse 25: "Woe to you, teachers of the law and Pharisees, you hypocrites! You clean the outside of the cup and bowl, but inside they are full of greed and self-indulgence." Hypocrisy is the same as lying. It's just that in addition to lying to others, the person is also lying to themselves. Pride is definitely the main cause of hypocrisy.

What we need is greater accountability in our government, as well as in business and education. If we are to have enduring hope for our nation's future, then we must insist on greater transparency. In an earlier chapter, the story of Ananias and Sapphira in the book of Acts was referenced. This example of open transparency and accountability would be as unheard of today as an alien ship from Mars landing on the earth.

I believe that the only way we will ever see this increased level of transparency and accountability is when "we the people" start getting more involved and start speaking out boldly, declaring the truth in love. Ephesians 4:14–16 (NIV) says,

> Then we will no longer be infants, tossed
> back and forth by the waves, and blown here and

there by every wind of teaching and by the cunning and craftiness of people in their deceitful scheming. Instead, speaking the truth in love, we will grow to become in every respect the mature body of Him who is the head, that is, Christ. From Him, the whole body, joined and held together by every supporting ligament, grows and builds itself up in love, as each part does its work.

Obviously, in our centuries-old election process where we exercise our right and obligation to vote, we find a measure of control in affecting change. However, it's not enough. There are more unabating means of affecting change other than simply on election day every two years. First and foremost, we can return to the paradigm our Founding Fathers modeled, which was the citizen acting as a public servant; for example, the businessman or woman, doctor, minister, or educator, perhaps, serving as an elected official, not as a career politician since we already have too many of those now, but rather, on a short-term basis, with more of us taking our turns.

It doesn't have to be just on the large national level either. Firstly, run for a local position such as city council, school board member, mayor, or state legislator. Secondly, be involved in a charitable organization that gives back to the community. Perhaps consider starting a regular prayer meeting at your home with the focus being on prayer for our nation and your respective city and state. These are ways we can ensure the direction our nation is heading in the future is in line with the principles and values our Founding Fathers and, more importantly, God Almighty established for us.

Another change desperately needed is the proper vetting of our candidates before they are even given the opportunity to run for office. Think about how a large corporation goes through a very rigorous and fastidious process before naming even the candidates for the position of manager or, especially, CEO. Why shouldn't a nation insist on the same background screening and lengthy interview process before we allow that person to be in a position to be elected to political office, where they will make quality-of-life-determining decisions? Instead, in recent years, we've elected certain people to office who seem "hell-bent" on transforming our country into another China or Venezuela.

We must stop this pernicious trend before we all wake up one day and discover we can no longer enjoy the same freedoms and rights. I am not advocating at all for what happened in the early '50s with the McCarthy witch-hunt trials in search of communist threats. Thank God, President Eisenhower finally stepped in, albeit a little late, and brought about a decisive end to that egregious attack on the First and Fifth Amendments.

We must always remember and teach our children sedulously that many men and women have made the ultimate sacrifice, their very lives, to protect and ensure those freedoms and rights. Reinstating the Pledge of Allegiance (with "under God") being recited daily in our schools would be a very good start!

Thomas Jefferson once wrote, "The tree of liberty must be refreshed from time to time with the blood of patriots and tyrants." Lord knows we've shed enough blood on distant shores as well as our own soil already. At what point will all of us as patriots rise up and say no more? The covenant is too important, the price already paid too great, and the future altogether too tenuous to sit by complacent, naive, or, worse yet, indifferent.

As stated at the onset of this chapter, "Hope deferred makes the heart sick." Our nation's heart and its citizens' are sick. We're sick of watching broken promises, sick of waiting for equal justice to be served, and sick of being told to trust in people who clearly want to lead only for self-serving gain and power.

The Bible tells us that the enemy prowls around looking for an opportunity to devour. I think most of us would agree that when COVID happened, it presented an opportunity for those without integrity or sincerity to impose draconian measures to gain control over society. It was far greater an offense than a mere officious act, yet no less nefarious than the impressment during the War of 1812. It was a premeditated and conceived attempt to alter the political and spiritual landscape of our nation forever.

Those of us committed to keeping the covenant with God and protecting our nation's future must pray for wisdom and discernment to recognize these insidious strategies. Otherwise, we could find ourselves beyond hope in the not-too-distant future. Ralph Waldo Emerson once wrote, "The Americans have many virtues, but they have not Faith and Hope. I know no two words whose meaning is more lost sight of." Let us strive together in the future to come united in the common cause of preserving our rich heritage and covenant with God to prove Emerson wrong.

We have to be willing to fight for those values to be evident in our nation once again. I am speaking of a fight that takes place primarily on our knees, crying out to the living God for His divine intervention and healing. First and foremost, there must be a purifying of our hearts which entails forgiveness of others, forgiveness of ourselves, and acknowledgment of our desperate need for God's forgiveness.

I have heard many speak of the need for a splitting of our nation into two separate countries, one for the conservatives and one for the liberals. And on face value, that may seem like the easy way out of this situation we're in. However, in the long run, it would be much better to reconcile the whole nation back to God and back to the covenant and way of life that have sustained us for so many years as a people. For comparison, to see the effect the splintering of a nation has on its people, we need not look further than Israel splitting into the Northern Kingdom of Israel and the Southern Kingdom of Judah, or even more recently on what happened to this great land and the heart of this nation during the devasting Civil War.

Recovery and healing can take centuries, if they happen at all, when a nation is split into two just as when a marriage is split, fractured into two pieces of what was once whole and complete. I realize sometimes this severing of one into two must take place, as in the case of our nation breaking off from Great Britain. However, there was a logistical piece of that which made the severing logical and perspicuous. If our nation today were to split into two separate nations because of our sharing of one contiguous land, the resulting confusion and detriment would be felt for decades and may never even reach a final resolution.

We must always consider the cost of disunion. Albeit totally justified and worthwhile, the Revolutionary War had a devastating and protracted effect. To glamorize that war, or any war, and what our brave men sacrificed would be a grave injustice. Having said that, it's also important to remember and honor what the brave ones who went before us have done to bring and keep this nation in existence.

> You know the rest. In the books you have read, How the British Regulars fired and fled,—How the farmers gave them ball for ball, From behind each fence and farm-yard wall, Chasing the red-coats down the lane, Then crossing the fields to emerge again Under the trees at the turn of the road, And only pausing to fire and load.
>
> So through the night rode Paul Revere; And so through the night went his cry of alarm To every Middlesex village and farm,—A cry of defiance and not of fear, A voice in the darkness, a knock at the door, And a word that shall echo forevermore! For, borne on the night-wind of the Past, Through all our history, to the last, In the hour of darkness and peril and need, The people will waken and listen to hear The hurrying hoof-beats of that steed, And the midnight message of Paul Revere. (*The Complete Poetical Works of Henry Wadsworth Longfellow, 1903*)

Just like the timeless message of what happened that courageous night as our nation was being born, so also today, the battle cry is the same:

God's people who acknowledge His holy name and pledge their lives to His everlasting fame, rise up and stand firm in His glory and right, and be now resolved to this laudable fight!

Author's Request

If you have enjoyed reading this simple reminder and sense the LORD stirring in your heart to act accordingly, please share this book with a friend or relative. It is my sincere hope and prayer that as you do, the vision and calling God has entrusted us all with of reaffirming our nation's commitment to the Almighty will spread like a holy fire throughout our land and lead to the revival and renewal that Ronald Reagan and so many other leaders from our past desired. It is imperative that we act while there's still time. The hour is near, and the time is now to humble ourselves and seek His face. God reminds us, as His people, "We should look for the LORD before it's too late; we should call to Him while He is still near" (Isaiah 55:6).

About the Author

David L. Mahan is a graduate of ministry from Wagner Leadership Institute (a.k.a. Wagner University). He is married and is the father of one son and five grandchildren. Dave is also the founder of Ezekiel Prayer Ministries and calls Arizona home. His passion is prayer and worship, as well as American history. Dave loves to help others realize their full potential in God's calling for their lives.